Why things don't work
HELICOPTER

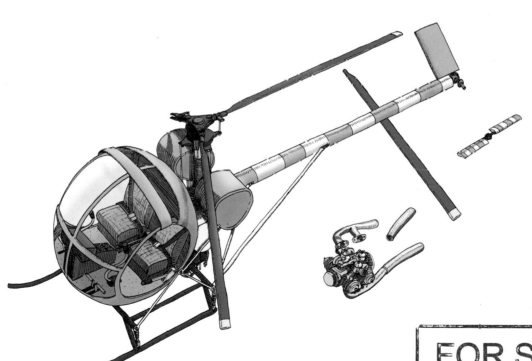

www.raintreepublishers.co.uk
Visit our website to find out more information about
Raintree books.

To order:
☎ Phone 44 (0) 1865 888112
▤ Send a fax to 44 (0) 1865 314091
▢ Visit the Raintree bookshop at
www.raintreepublishers.co.uk to browse our
catalogue and order online.

Why things don't work HELICOPTER
was produced by

David West ⚥ Children's Books
7 Princeton Court
55 Felsham Road
London SW15 1AZ

Editor: Dominique Crowley
Consultant: William Moore

First published in Great Britain by
Raintree, Halley Court, Jordan Hill, Oxford OX2 8EJ, part of
Harcourt Education. Raintree is a registered trademark of Harcourt
Education Ltd.

13 digit ISBN: 978 1 4062 0550 3

11 10 09 08 07
10 9 8 7 6 5 4 3 2 1

British Library Cataloguing in Publication Data

West, David
  Helicopter. - (Why things don't work)
  1.Helicopters - Comic books, strips, etc. - Juvenile
  literature
  I.Title
  629.1'33352'0288

Printed and bound in China

Why things don't work
HELICOPTER
by David West

Contents

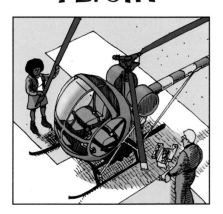

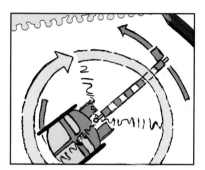

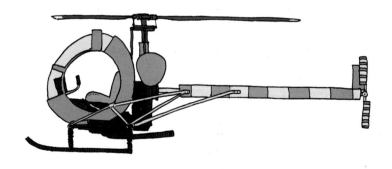

Cousin Ed's helicopter

ANNIE HAS RECENTLY PASSED HER HELICOPTER FLYING TEST. HER COUSIN, ED, HAS AGREED TO LET HER FLY HIS HELICOPTER IF SHE HELPS HIM MEND IT. AT THE MOMENT, IT IS ON HIS HELIPAD WITH NO FUEL IN THE TANK.

ALSO, THERE SEEM TO BE A FEW OTHER PROBLEMS...

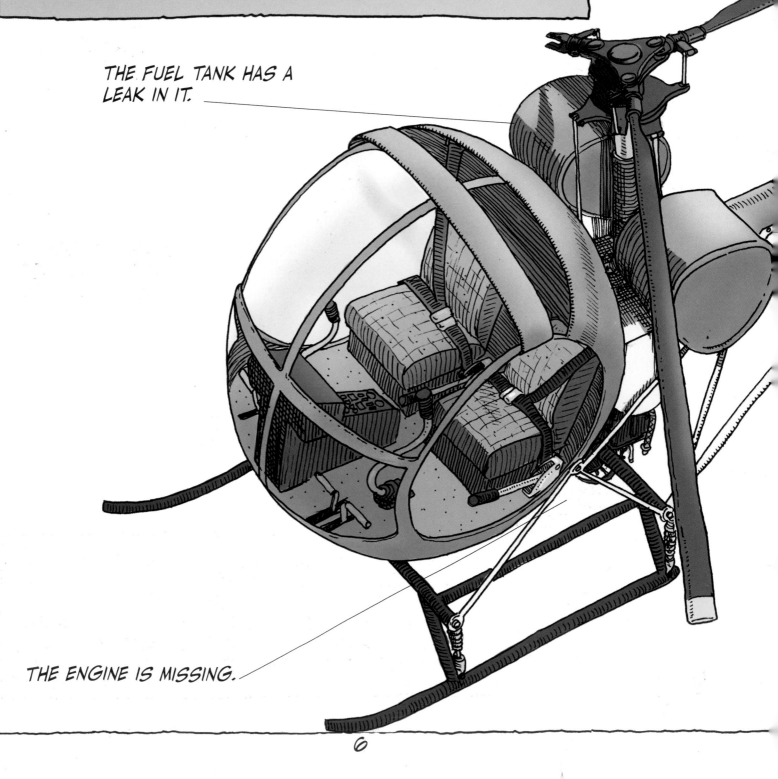

THE FUEL TANK HAS A LEAK IN IT.

THE ENGINE IS MISSING.

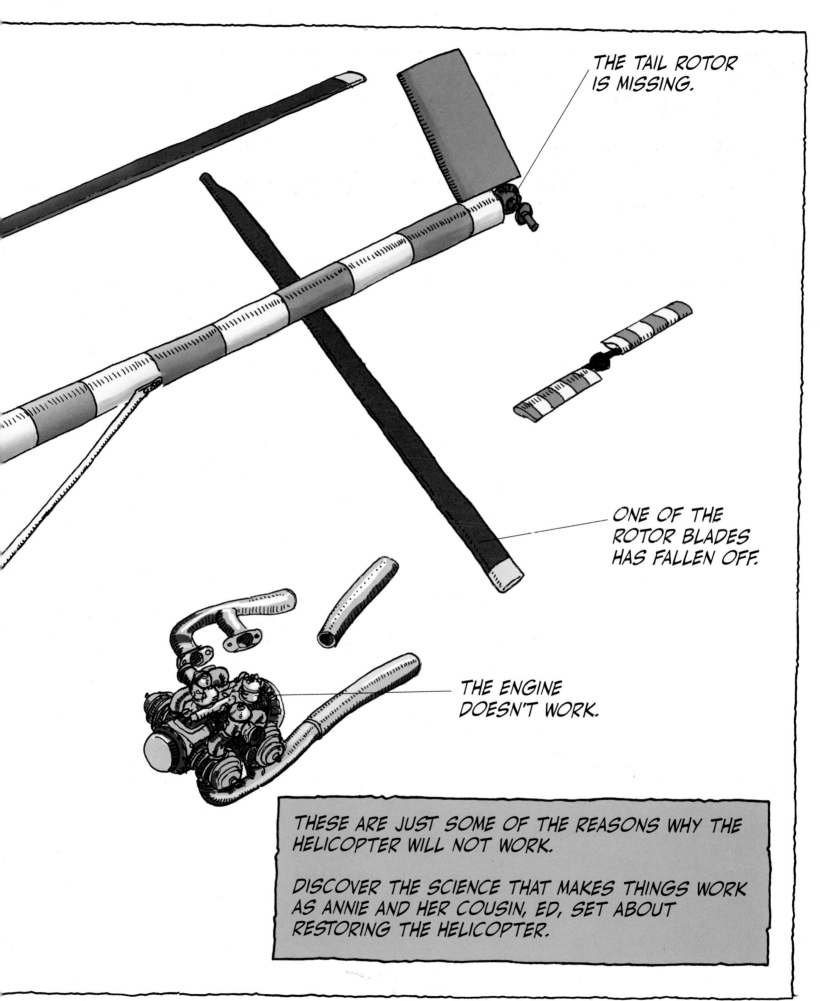

THE TAIL ROTOR IS MISSING.

ONE OF THE ROTOR BLADES HAS FALLEN OFF.

THE ENGINE DOESN'T WORK.

THESE ARE JUST SOME OF THE REASONS WHY THE HELICOPTER WILL NOT WORK.

DISCOVER THE SCIENCE THAT MAKES THINGS WORK AS ANNIE AND HER COUSIN, ED, SET ABOUT RESTORING THE HELICOPTER.

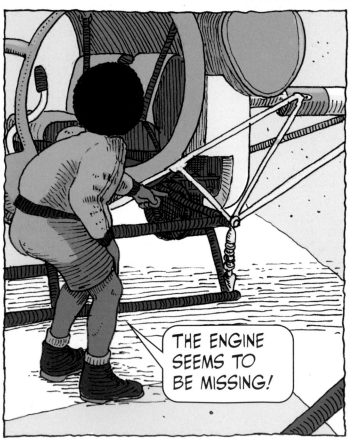

IT'S A FLAT FOUR PISTON ENGINE.

WHAT'S A FLAT FOUR PISTON ENGINE?

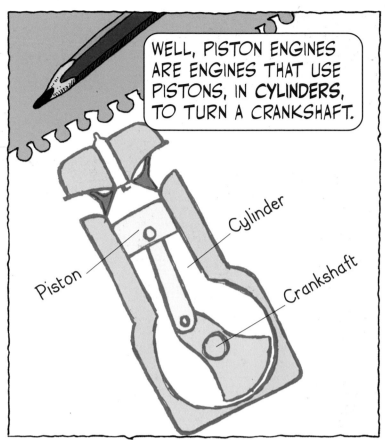

WELL, PISTON ENGINES ARE ENGINES THAT USE PISTONS, IN **CYLINDERS**, TO TURN A CRANKSHAFT.

Piston

Cylinder

Crankshaft

IN A NORMAL ENGINE THERE ARE USUALLY FOUR CYLINDERS ARRANGED IN A LINE.

SOME ENGINE DESIGNS HAVE THE CYLINDERS ARRANGED IN A V-SHAPE. AND SOME HAVE SIX, EIGHT, TEN, OR EVEN TWELVE CYLINDERS.

IN A FLAT FOUR THERE ARE FOUR CYLINDERS THAT ARE LYING DOWN.

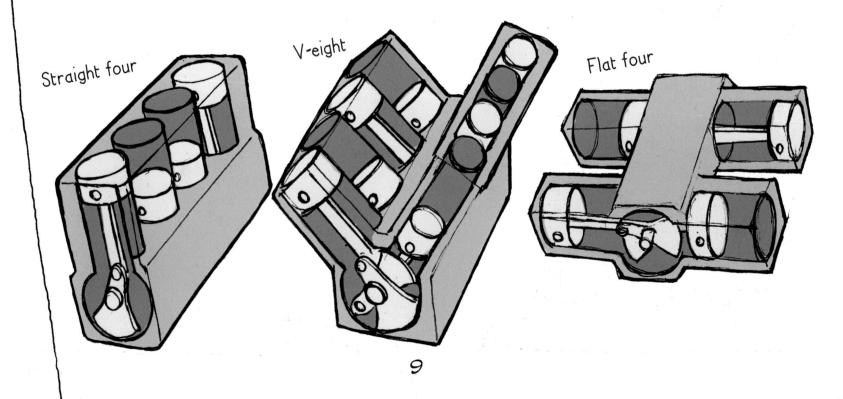

Straight four

V-eight

Flat four

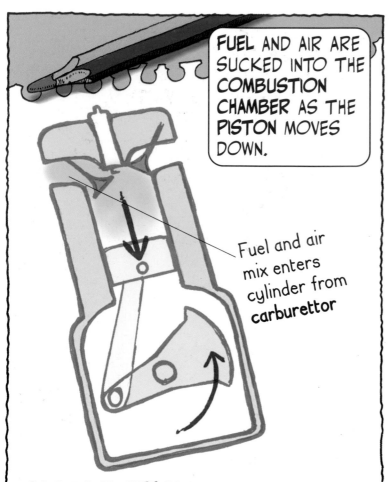

FUEL AND AIR ARE SUCKED INTO THE COMBUSTION CHAMBER AS THE PISTON MOVES DOWN.

Fuel and air mix enters cylinder from **carburettor**

AS THE PISTON MOVES UP, IT SQUEEZES THE AIR/FUEL MIXTURE.

Fuel and air mix is squashed

A **SPARK PLUG** CAUSES THE AIR/FUEL MIXTURE TO EXPLODE, FORCING THE PISTON DOWN.

A spark from the spark plug makes the fuel and air mixture explode

Exhaust gases are forced out

WHEN THE PISTON RETURNS, IT FORCES THE **EXHAUST GASES** OUT. THEN THE WHOLE PROCESS STARTS AGAIN.

EXCEPT, IN THIS CASE, IT DOESN'T. LOOK AT THAT. THE OIL HAS LEAKED OUT FROM A CRACK AND THE WHOLE ENGINE HAS SEIZED UP.

WHY?

OIL MAKES THE SURFACES OF THE MOVING PARTS SLIPPERY. THIS HELPS REDUCE **FRICTION**, WHICH CREATES A LOT OF HEAT.

RUB YOUR HANDS TOGETHER. CAN YOU FEEL THE HEAT BUILD UP?

YES.

THAT'S WHAT HAPPENED TO THIS ENGINE. IT GOT SO HOT, THE PARTS OVERHEATED AND JAMMED. THIS BROKE THE ENGINE.

CAN IT BE REPAIRED?

NO. IT'S TOO BADLY DAMAGED.

LUCKILY, I GOT THIS FROM A SCRAPYARD. IT'S A WANKEL ROTARY ENGINE.

WOW. HOW MANY CYLINDERS DOES IT HAVE?

IT DOESN'T HAVE ANY CYLINDERS! IT WORKS DIFFERENTLY FROM A PISTON ENGINE.

SEE THIS TRIANGULAR PART? IT SPINS ROUND. NONE OF THE PARTS GO UP AND DOWN AS THEY WOULD IN A PISTON ENGINE.

AIR AND FUEL ENTER HERE.

Fuel and air mixture from the carburettor

AS THE TRIANGULAR ROTOR ROTATES, THE FUEL/AIR MIX IS SQUASHED.

THE SPARK PLUG **IGNITES** THE FUEL/AIR MIX, WITH A SPARK. THE EXPLODING GASES EXPAND, FORCING THE TRIANGLE AROUND.

Spark plug

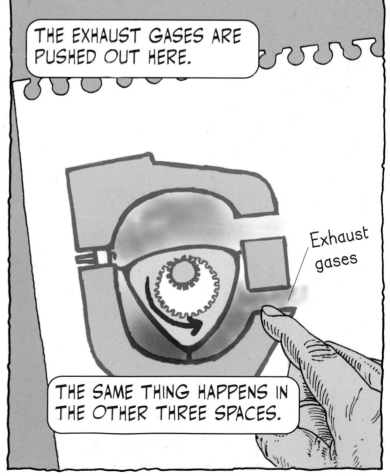

THE EXHAUST GASES ARE PUSHED OUT HERE.

Exhaust gases

THE SAME THING HAPPENS IN THE OTHER THREE SPACES.

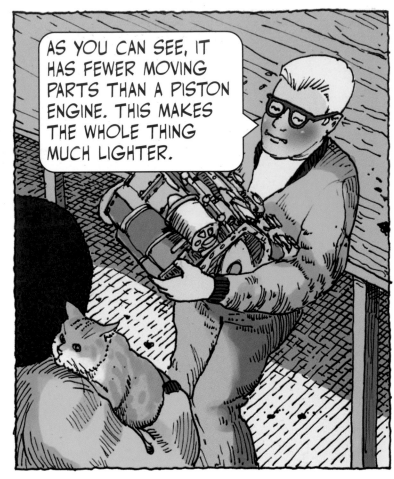

WHICH WAY UP DOES IT GO?

THIS WAY. IT'S JUST LIKE A PLANE'S WING.

Lift

Low air pressure area

Faster moving air

Rotor blade **cross-section**

AS THE BLADE TURNS, THE AIR RUSHING OVER THE TOP SURFACE GOES FASTER, AS IT HAS FURTHER TO TRAVEL THAN THE AIR TRAVELLING UNDERNEATH.

Slower moving air

THIS CREATES AN AREA OF **LOW AIR PRESSURE** ABOVE THE BLADE. THE BLADE MOVES INTO THIS AREA, PULLING THE REST OF THE HELICOPTER WITH IT.

TO SEE HOW THIS WORKS, IMAGINE THIS PIECE OF PAPER IS THE CURVED EDGE OF A WING.

WHEN I BLOW OVER THE TOP, THE SPEEDING AIR SHOULD MAKE IT LIFT UP.

WOW!

THAT'S RIGHT. AS THE SWASH PLATE MOVES, IT PUSHES THESE **PITCH ARM RODS** UP OR DOWN.

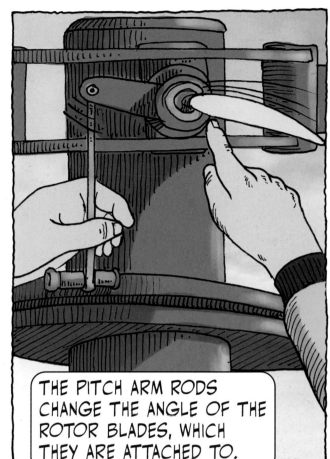

THE PITCH ARM RODS CHANGE THE ANGLE OF THE ROTOR BLADES, WHICH THEY ARE ATTACHED TO.

WHAT DOES THAT DO?

THE STEEPER THE BLADE'S ANGLE, THE MORE LIFT IT PROVIDES.

THIS MEANS YOU CAN TILT THE HELICOPTER IN ANY DIRECTION BY TILTING THE SWASH PLATE.

More lift

Blade faces up

Helicopter tilts left

Negative lift

Blade faces down

Helicopter tilts forwards

17

IF THE WHOLE SWASH PLATE IS RAISED, ALL THE BLADES TWIST AT THE SAME ANGLE. THIS WILL CREATE LIFT ON ALL THE BLADES AT THE SAME TIME...

...WHICH MAKES THE HELICOPTER GO STRAIGHT UP.

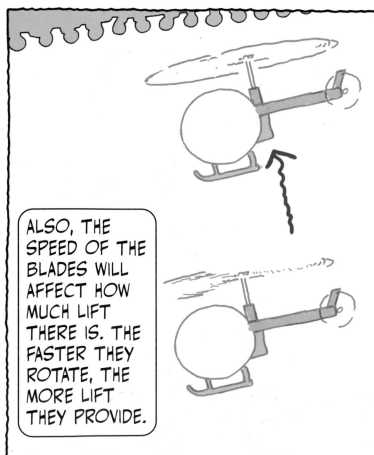

ALSO, THE SPEED OF THE BLADES WILL AFFECT HOW MUCH LIFT THERE IS. THE FASTER THEY ROTATE, THE MORE LIFT THEY PROVIDE.

THE BLADES FEEL A BIT WOBBLY.

YES, THEY'RE MEANT TO.

THE BLADES ACTUALLY BEND AS THEY ROTATE. THIS SOLVES A PROBLEM YOU WOULD GET IF THEY WERE **RIGID**.

IN ORDER TO STOP THIS, THE BLADES GOING FORWARDS BEND UP, WHICH REDUCES THEIR LIFT.

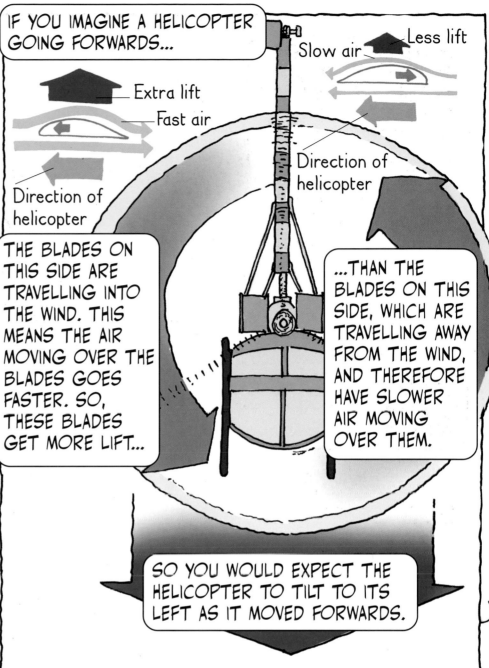

IF YOU IMAGINE A HELICOPTER GOING FORWARDS...

Extra lift

Fast air

Direction of helicopter

Slow air

Less lift

Direction of helicopter

THE BLADES ON THIS SIDE ARE TRAVELLING INTO THE WIND. THIS MEANS THE AIR MOVING OVER THE BLADES GOES FASTER. SO, THESE BLADES GET MORE LIFT...

...THAN THE BLADES ON THIS SIDE, WHICH ARE TRAVELLING AWAY FROM THE WIND, AND THEREFORE HAVE SLOWER AIR MOVING OVER THEM.

SO YOU WOULD EXPECT THE HELICOPTER TO TILT TO ITS LEFT AS IT MOVED FORWARDS.

Blade bends up, cancelling out extra lift

Blade bends down, which creates more lift

THE BLADES GOING BACKWARDS BEND DOWN LIKE A BIRD'S WING, WHICH CREATES EXTRA LIFT. THIS EVENS OUT ANY DIFFERENCE IN AIR SPEED OVER THE ROTOR BLADES.

OH DEAR. HERE'S OUR PROBLEM. THERE'S NO TAIL ROTOR.

WHAT DOES IT DO?

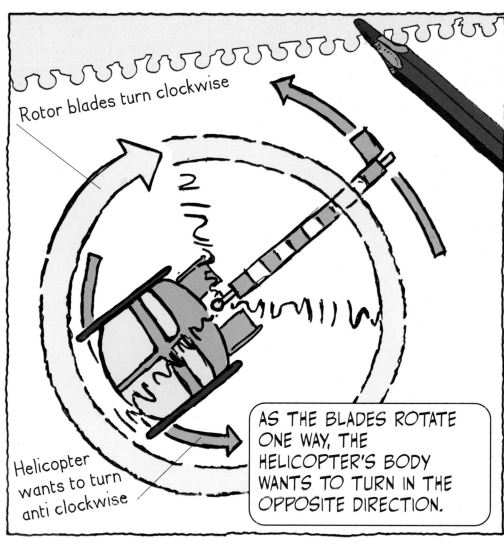

Rotor blades turn clockwise

Helicopter wants to turn anti clockwise

AS THE BLADES ROTATE ONE WAY, THE HELICOPTER'S BODY WANTS TO TURN IN THE OPPOSITE DIRECTION.

SIT IN THIS SWIVEL CHAIR AND TRY TO SPIN ROUND WITHOUT TOUCHING ANYTHING.

WHOA.

YOU SEE, AS YOUR TOP HALF WANTS TO GO ONE WAY, THE BOTTOM HALF WANTS TO GO THE OTHER WAY.

THIS IS WHAT HAPPENS TO A HELICOPTER WITHOUT A TAIL ROTOR.

THE TAIL ROTOR IS ATTACHED TO THE MAIN ENGINE THROUGH A GEARBOX.

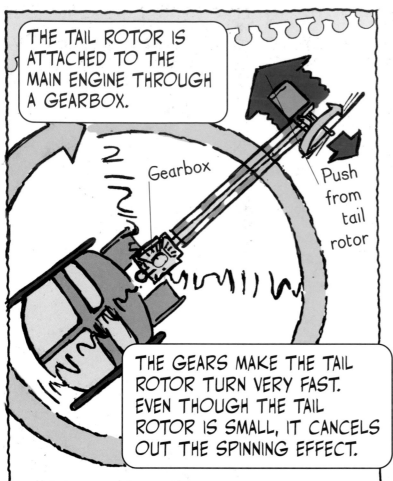

Gearbox

Push from tail rotor

THE GEARS MAKE THE TAIL ROTOR TURN VERY FAST. EVEN THOUGH THE TAIL ROTOR IS SMALL, IT CANCELS OUT THE SPINNING EFFECT.

WE FIXED THE TAIL ROTOR ON ITS **AXLE** AT THE END.

I'LL JUST GO AND CLEAN UP AND THEN WE'LL TAKE OUT THE HELICOPTER FOR A TEST FLIGHT.

HELLO, WHAT'S YOUR NAME?

DOMINIQUE. WHAT'S YOURS?

ANNIE.

ARE YOU GOING TO FLY ED'S HELICOPTER?

YES.

23

WHUPPA
WHUPPA
WHUPPA

WHUPPA
WHUPPA
WHUPPA

LET DOWN THE PITCH CONTROL LEVER A BIT TO STOP CLIMBING.

PUSH THE CYCLIC CONTROL LEVER FORWARDS AND LIFT THE PITCH CONTROL LEVER.

WE MOVED FORWARDS.

I PUSHED THE LEFT FOOT PEDAL TO POINT WEST AND PULLED THE PITCH CONTROL LEVER TO GAIN HEIGHT.

WHUPPA

WHUPPA

WHUPPA

WE HOVERED FOR A WHILE. HOVERING IS QUITE DIFFICULT AS YOU HAVE TO CONTROL ALL THE LEVERS AND PEDALS AT THE SAME TIME.

I CAN SEE YOUR CARAVAN.

WHUPPA WHUPPA WHUPPA

DWEEEEP

SUDDENLY, A WARNING LIGHT CAME ON.

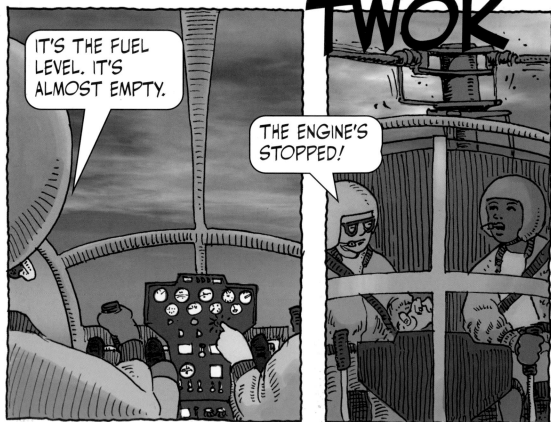

IT'S THE FUEL LEVEL. IT'S ALMOST EMPTY.

TWOK

THE ENGINE'S STOPPED!

26

I TRIED TO REMEMBER EMERGENCY PROCEDURE FROM MY LESSONS, PUTTING US INTO A DIVE. THE AIR RACING OVER THE BLADES KEPT THEM ROTATING.

SWISH SWISH SWISH

THAT FIELD LOOKS GOOD TO LAND IN.

JUST BEFORE WE HIT THE GROUND I PULLED UP THE NOSE USING THE PITCH CONTROL LEVER AND THE CYCLIC CONTROL STICK.

HOLD ON!

THE FREELY ROTATING BLADES CREATED ENOUGH LIFT FOR THE HELICOPTER TO SLOW TO NORMAL LANDING SPEED.

SWISH SWISH SWISH

WE LANDED WITH A FAINT BUMP.

SWISH

NICE LANDING.

IT TURNED OUT THERE WAS A LEAK IN THE FUEL TANK. WE SOON HAD IT PATCHED UP AND, THE FOLLOWING WEEK, WE FLEW TO AN AIR SHOW IN THE HELICOPTER.

WHUPPA

WHUPPA

WHUPPA

WE SAW A TWIN-ROTOR HELICOPTER CALLED A CHINOOK.

HEY, THAT HELICOPTER HAS NO TAIL ROTOR.

IT DOESN'T NEED ONE. THE SECOND ROTOR ROTATES IN THE OPPOSITE DIRECTION, WHICH HAS THE SAME EFFECT.

LOOK! THIS ONE DOES THE SAME THING BUT ONE ROTOR SITS ABOVE THE OTHER.

I'M NOT SURE IF I'D WANT TO DO THAT.

THEY HAVE TO IF THEY ARE RESCUING SOMEONE AT SEA.

THERE WAS A HUGE RUSSIAN GUNSHIP...

IT'S CALLED A HIND.

...AND AN AMAZING DISPLAY BY AN APACHE HELICOPTER.

WOW! IT CAN DO A LOOP.

WE SAW A CROSS BETWEEN A PLANE AND A HELICOPTER. THE ENGINES TILTED UPWARDS SO IT COULD TAKE OFF AND LAND VERTICALLY.

IT'S CALLED AN OSPREY.

THE BEST BIT WAS HAVING A RIDE IN A GYROCOPTER. IT HAD A PROPELLER TO POWER IT BUT THE ROTOR JUST TURNED FREELY TO GIVE LIFT.

IT FLIES JUST LIKE OUR HELICOPTER DID WHEN WE HAD THE EMERGENCY.

Parts of a helicopter

Rotor head

Rotor blades

Cockpit

Swash plate

Tail rotor

Fuel tank

Cyclic
control
stick

Gearbox

Pitch
control
lever

Engine

Tail rotor

Rotor head

Rotor blades

Swash plate

Instrument
panel

Cyclic
control
sticks

Fuel tanks

Rotor head

Instrument
panel

Rotor blades

Pedals

Cyclic
control
sticks

Glossary

AXLE
A METAL ROD OR PIN ON WHICH A SPINNING OBJECT SUCH AS A WHEEL OR ROTOR BLADE IS ATTACHED

CARBURETTOR
PART OF AN ENGINE THAT MIXES FUEL AND AIR TOGETHER BEFORE THEY ENTER THE COMBUSTION CHAMBER

COMBUSTION CHAMBER
TOP PART OF THE CYLINDER WHERE THE FUEL/AIR MIXTURE IS IGNITED BY THE SPARK PLUG

CROSS-SECTION
THE SHAPE SHOWN OF AN OBJECT WHEN IT IS SLICED THROUGH BY AN IMAGINARY BLADE

CYLINDER
THE METAL SLEEVE INSIDE WHICH A PISTON MOVES

EXHAUST GASES
GASES CREATED BY THE EXPLODING FUEL/AIR MIXTURE IN THE ENGINE

FRICTION
THE RESISTANCE TO MOVEMENT THAT OCCURS WHEN TWO SURFACES RUB AGAINST EACH OTHER, CREATING HEAT

FUEL
MATERIAL THAT IS BURNED FOR POWER. HELICOPTER FUEL IS MADE FROM OIL.

GEARBOX
THE HOUSING FOR THE GEARS

IGNITE
TO SET FIRE TO

LOW AIR PRESSURE AREA
AN AREA OF AIR THAT HAS LESS AIR THAN ITS SURROUNDING AREA

PISTON
A SOLID CYLINDER THAT MOVES TO AND FRO INSIDE ANOTHER CYLINDER

PITCH ARM ROD
A METAL ROD ATTACHED BY JOINTS TO THE SWASH PLATE AND THE ROTOR BLADE. AS IT MOVES UP OR DOWN, IT CHANGES THE PITCH, OR ANGLE, OF THE ROTOR BLADE.

RIGID
FIRM AND UNBENDING

ROTATE
TURN

SPARK PLUG
A PART IN THE TOP OF AN ENGINE'S CYLINDER THAT CREATES AN ELECTRIC SPARK TO IGNITE THE FUEL/AIR MIXTURE

SWASH PLATE
TWO LARGE METAL DISCS, ONE ON TOP OF THE OTHER, BELOW THE ROTOR HEAD

THROTTLE
THE CONTROL THAT MAKES AN ENGINE RUN QUICKER OR SLOWER

Index